Deam Journal

Date:__________ Time:___

Thoughts Before Sleep

Emotions Before Sleep

Dream

Interpretation

Feeling Upon Awakening

Comments

Deam Journal

Date:__________ Time:__________

Thoughts Before Sleep

Emotions Before Sleep

Dream

Interpretation

Feeling Upon Awakening

Comments

Deam Journal

Date:__________ Time:__________

Thoughts Before Sleep

Emotions Before Sleep

Dream

Interpretation

Feeling Upon Awakening

Comments

Deam Journal

Date:____________ Time:____________

Thoughts Before Sleep

Emotions Before Sleep

Dream

Interpretation

Feeling Upon Awakening

Comments

Deam Journal

Date:____________ Time:____________

Thoughts Before Sleep

Emotions Before Sleep

Dream

Interpretation

Feeling Upon Awakening

Comments

Deam Journal

Date:____________ Time:____________

Thoughts Before Sleep

Emotions Before Sleep

Dream

Interpretation

Feeling Upon Awakening

Comments

Deam Journal

Date:____________ Time:____________

Thoughts Before Sleep

Emotions Before Sleep

Dream

Interpretation

Feeling Upon Awakening

Comments

Deam Journal

Date:____________ Time:____________

Thoughts Before Sleep

Emotions Before Sleep

Dream

Interpretation

Feeling Upon Awakening

Comments

Deam Journal

Date:____________ Time:____________

Thoughts Before Sleep

Emotions Before Sleep

Dream

Interpretation

Feeling Upon Awakening

Comments

Deam Journal

Date:____________ Time:____________

Thoughts Before Sleep

Emotions Before Sleep

Dream

Interpretation

Feeling Upon Awakening

Comments

Deam Journal

Date:__________ Time:__________

Thoughts Before Sleep

Emotions Before Sleep

Dream

Interpretation

Feeling Upon Awakening

Comments

Deam Journal

Date:____________ Time:____________

Thoughts Before Sleep

Emotions Before Sleep

Dream

Interpretation

Feeling Upon Awakening

Comments

Deam Journal

Date:______________ Time:______________

Thoughts Before Sleep

Emotions Before Sleep

Dream

Interpretation

Feeling Upon Awakening

Comments

Deam Journal

Date:____________ Time:____________

Thoughts Before Sleep

Emotions Before Sleep

Dream

Interpretation

Feeling Upon Awakening

Comments

Deam Journal

Date:__________ Time:__________

Thoughts Before Sleep

Emotions Before Sleep

Dream

Interpretation

Feeling Upon Awakening

Comments

Deam Journal

Date:____________ Time:____________

Thoughts Before Sleep

Emotions Before Sleep

Dream

Interpretation

Feeling Upon Awakening

Comments

Deam Journal

Date:____________ Time:____________

Thoughts Before Sleep

Emotions Before Sleep

Dream

Interpretation

Feeling Upon Awakening

Comments

Deam Journal

Date:__________ Time:__________

Thoughts Before Sleep

Emotions Before Sleep

Dream

Interpretation

Feeling Upon Awakening

Comments

Deam Journal

Date:____________ Time:____________

Thoughts Before Sleep

Emotions Before Sleep

Dream

Interpretation

Feeling Upon Awakening

Comments

Deam Journal

Date:____________ Time:____________

Thoughts Before Sleep

Emotions Before Sleep

Dream

Interpretation

Feeling Upon Awakening

Comments

Deam Journal

Date:__________ Time:__________

Thoughts Before Sleep

Emotions Before Sleep

Dream

Interpretation

Feeling Upon Awakening

Comments

Deam Journal

Date:____________ Time:____________

Thoughts Before Sleep

Emotions Before Sleep

Dream

Interpretation

Feeling Upon Awakening

Comments

Deam Journal

Date:____________ Time:____________

Thoughts Before Sleep

Emotions Before Sleep

Dream

Interpretation

Feeling Upon Awakening

Comments

Deam Journal

Date:____________ Time:____________

Thoughts Before Sleep

Emotions Before Sleep

Dream

Interpretation

Feeling Upon Awakening

Comments

Deam Journal

Date:____________ Time:____________

Thoughts Before Sleep

Emotions Before Sleep

Dream

Interpretation

Feeling Upon Awakening

Comments

Deam Journal

Date:__________ Time:__________

Thoughts Before Sleep

Emotions Before Sleep

Dream

Interpretation

Feeling Upon Awakening

Comments

Deam Journal

Date:__________ Time:__________

Thoughts Before Sleep

Emotions Before Sleep

Dream

Interpretation

Feeling Upon Awakening

Comments

Deam Journal

Date:____________ Time:____________

Thoughts Before Sleep

Emotions Before Sleep

Dream

Interpretation

Feeling Upon Awakening

Comments

Deam Journal

Date:____________ Time:____________

Thoughts Before Sleep

Emotions Before Sleep

Dream

Interpretation

Feeling Upon Awakening

Comments

Deam Journal

Date:____________ Time:____________

Thoughts Before Sleep

Emotions Before Sleep

Dream

Interpretation

Feeling Upon Awakening

Comments

Deam Journal

Date:____________ Time:____________

Thoughts Before Sleep

Emotions Before Sleep

Dream

Interpretation

Feeling Upon Awakening

Comments

Deam Journal

Date:______________ Time:______________

Thoughts Before Sleep

Emotions Before Sleep

Dream

Interpretation

Feeling Upon Awakening

Comments

Deam Journal

Date:____________ Time:____________

Thoughts Before Sleep

Emotions Before Sleep

Dream

Interpretation

Feeling Upon Awakening

Comments

Deam Journal

Date:____________ Time:____________

Thoughts Before Sleep

Emotions Before Sleep

Dream

Interpretation

Feeling Upon Awakening

Comments

Deam Journal

Date:____________ Time:____________

Thoughts Before Sleep

Emotions Before Sleep

Dream

Interpretation

Feeling Upon Awakening

Comments

Deam Journal

Date:__________ Time:__________

Thoughts Before Sleep

Emotions Before Sleep

Dream

Interpretation

Feeling Upon Awakening

Comments

Deam Journal

Date:____________ Time:____________

Thoughts Before Sleep

Emotions Before Sleep

Dream

Interpretation

Feeling Upon Awakening

Comments

Deam Journal

Date:____________ Time:____________

Thoughts Before Sleep

Emotions Before Sleep

Dream

Interpretation

Feeling Upon Awakening

Comments

Deam Journal

Date:____________ Time:____________

Thoughts Before Sleep

Emotions Before Sleep

Dream

Interpretation

Feeling Upon Awakening

Comments

Deam Journal

Date:____________ Time:____________

Thoughts Before Sleep

Emotions Before Sleep

Dream

Interpretation

Feeling Upon Awakening

Comments

Deam Journal

Date:____________ Time:____________

Thoughts Before Sleep

Emotions Before Sleep

Dream

Interpretation

Feeling Upon Awakening

Comments

Deam Journal

Date:____________ Time:____________

Thoughts Before Sleep

Emotions Before Sleep

Dream

Interpretation

Feeling Upon Awakening

Comments

Deam Journal

Date:____________ Time:____________

Thoughts Before Sleep

Emotions Before Sleep

Dream

Interpretation

Feeling Upon Awakening

Comments

Deam Journal

Date:____________ Time:____________

Thoughts Before Sleep

Emotions Before Sleep

Dream

Interpretation

Feeling Upon Awakening

Comments

Deam Journal

Date:____________ Time:____________

Thoughts Before Sleep

Emotions Before Sleep

Dream

Interpretation

Feeling Upon Awakening

Comments

Deam Journal

Date:____________ Time:____________

Thoughts Before Sleep

Emotions Before Sleep

Dream

Interpretation

Feeling Upon Awakening

Comments

Deam Journal

Date:__________ Time:__________

Thoughts Before Sleep

Emotions Before Sleep

Dream

Interpretation

Feeling Upon Awakening

Comments

Deam Journal

Date:____________ Time:____________

Thoughts Before Sleep

Emotions Before Sleep

Dream

Interpretation

Feeling Upon Awakening

Comments

Deam Journal

Date:____________ Time:____________

Thoughts Before Sleep

Emotions Before Sleep

Dream

Interpretation

Feeling Upon Awakening

Comments

Deam Journal

Date:____________ Time:____________

Thoughts Before Sleep

Emotions Before Sleep

Dream

Interpretation

Feeling Upon Awakening

Comments

Deam Journal

Date:____________ Time:____________

Thoughts Before Sleep

Emotions Before Sleep

Dream

Interpretation

Feeling Upon Awakening

Comments

Deam Journal

Date:____________ Time:____________

Thoughts Before Sleep

Emotions Before Sleep

Dream

Interpretation

Feeling Upon Awakening

Comments

Deam Journal

Date:____________ Time:____________

Thoughts Before Sleep

Emotions Before Sleep

Dream

Interpretation

Feeling Upon Awakening

Comments

Deam Journal

Date:____________ Time:____________

Thoughts Before Sleep

Emotions Before Sleep

Dream

Interpretation

Feeling Upon Awakening

Comments

Deam Journal

Date:____________ Time:____________

Thoughts Before Sleep

Emotions Before Sleep

Dream

Interpretation

Feeling Upon Awakening

Comments

Deam Journal

Date:____________ Time:____________

Thoughts Before Sleep

Emotions Before Sleep

Dream

Interpretation

Feeling Upon Awakening

Comments

Deam Journal

Date:__________ Time:__________

Thoughts Before Sleep

Emotions Before Sleep

Dream

Interpretation

Feeling Upon Awakening

Comments

Deam Journal

Date:____________ Time:____________

Thoughts Before Sleep

Emotions Before Sleep

Dream

Interpretation

Feeling Upon Awakening

Comments

Deam Journal

Date:__________ Time:__________

Thoughts Before Sleep

Emotions Before Sleep

Dream

Interpretation

Feeling Upon Awakening

Comments

Deam Journal

Date:____________ Time:____________

Thoughts Before Sleep

Emotions Before Sleep

Dream

Interpretation

Feeling Upon Awakening

Comments

Deam Journal

Date:____________ Time:____________

Thoughts Before Sleep

Emotions Before Sleep

Dream

Interpretation

Feeling Upon Awakening

Comments

Deam Journal

Date:__________ Time:__________

Thoughts Before Sleep

Emotions Before Sleep

Dream

Interpretation

Feeling Upon Awakening

Comments

Deam Journal

Date:____________ Time:____________

Thoughts Before Sleep

Emotions Before Sleep

Dream

Interpretation

Feeling Upon Awakening

Comments

Deam Journal

Date:______________ Time:______________

Thoughts Before Sleep

Emotions Before Sleep

Dream

Interpretation

Feeling Upon Awakening

Comments

Deam Journal

Date:____________ Time:____________

Thoughts Before Sleep

Emotions Before Sleep

Dream

Interpretation

Feeling Upon Awakening

Comments

Deam Journal

Date:____________ Time:____________

Thoughts Before Sleep

Emotions Before Sleep

Dream

Interpretation

Feeling Upon Awakening

Comments

Deam Journal

Date:____________ Time:____________

Thoughts Before Sleep

Emotions Before Sleep

Dream

Interpretation

Feeling Upon Awakening

Comments

Deam Journal

Date:__________ Time:__________

Thoughts Before Sleep

Emotions Before Sleep

Dream

Interpretation

Feeling Upon Awakening

Comments

Deam Journal

Date:____________ Time:____________

Thoughts Before Sleep

Emotions Before Sleep

Dream

Interpretation

Feeling Upon Awakening

Comments

Deam Journal

Date:____________ Time:____________

Thoughts Before Sleep

Emotions Before Sleep

Dream

Interpretation

Feeling Upon Awakening

Comments

Deam Journal

Date:__________ Time:__________

Thoughts Before Sleep

Emotions Before Sleep

Dream

Interpretation

Feeling Upon Awakening

Comments

Deam Journal

Date:____________ Time:____________

Thoughts Before Sleep

Emotions Before Sleep

Dream

Interpretation

Feeling Upon Awakening

Comments

Deam Journal

Date:____________ Time:____________

Thoughts Before Sleep

Emotions Before Sleep

Dream

Interpretation

Feeling Upon Awakening

Comments

Deam Journal

Date:____________ Time:____________

Thoughts Before Sleep

Emotions Before Sleep

Dream

Interpretation

Feeling Upon Awakening

Comments

Deam Journal

Date:__________ Time:__________

Thoughts Before Sleep

Emotions Before Sleep

Dream

Interpretation

Feeling Upon Awakening

Comments

Deam Journal

Date:____________ Time:____________

Thoughts Before Sleep

Emotions Before Sleep

Dream

Interpretation

Feeling Upon Awakening

Comments

Deam Journal

Date:____________ Time:____________

Thoughts Before Sleep

Emotions Before Sleep

Dream

Interpretation

Feeling Upon Awakening

Comments

Deam Journal

Date:__________ Time:__________

Thoughts Before Sleep

Emotions Before Sleep

Dream

Interpretation

Feeling Upon Awakening

Comments

Deam Journal

Date:____________ Time:____________

Thoughts Before Sleep

Emotions Before Sleep

Dream

Interpretation

Feeling Upon Awakening

Comments

Deam Journal

Date:__________ Time:__________

Thoughts Before Sleep

Emotions Before Sleep

Dream

Interpretation

Feeling Upon Awakening

Comments

Deam Journal

Date:__________ Time:__________

Thoughts Before Sleep

Emotions Before Sleep

Dream

Interpretation

Feeling Upon Awakening

Comments

Deam Journal

Date:____________ Time:____________

Thoughts Before Sleep

Emotions Before Sleep

Dream

Interpretation

Feeling Upon Awakening

Comments

Deam Journal

Date:____________ Time:____________

Thoughts Before Sleep

Emotions Before Sleep

Dream

Interpretation

Feeling Upon Awakening

Comments

Deam Journal

Date:____________ Time:____________

Thoughts Before Sleep

Emotions Before Sleep

Dream

Interpretation

Feeling Upon Awakening

Comments

Deam Journal

Date:____________ Time:____________

Thoughts Before Sleep

Emotions Before Sleep

Dream

Interpretation

Feeling Upon Awakening

Comments

Deam Journal

Date:__________ Time:__________

Thoughts Before Sleep

Emotions Before Sleep

Dream

Interpretation

Feeling Upon Awakening

Comments

Deam Journal

Date:__________ Time:__________

Thoughts Before Sleep

Emotions Before Sleep

Dream

Interpretation

Feeling Upon Awakening

Comments

Deam Journal

Date:____________ Time:____________

Thoughts Before Sleep

Emotions Before Sleep

Dream

Interpretation

Feeling Upon Awakening

Comments

Deam Journal

Date:__________ Time:__________

Thoughts Before Sleep

Emotions Before Sleep

Dream

Interpretation

Feeling Upon Awakening

Comments

Deam Journal

Date:____________ Time:____________

Thoughts Before Sleep

Emotions Before Sleep

Dream

Interpretation

Feeling Upon Awakening

Comments

Deam Journal

Date:____________ Time:____________

Thoughts Before Sleep

Emotions Before Sleep

Dream

Interpretation

Feeling Upon Awakening

Comments

Deam Journal

Date:____________ Time:____________

Thoughts Before Sleep

Emotions Before Sleep

Dream

Interpretation

Feeling Upon Awakening

Comments

Deam Journal

Date:__________ Time:__________

Thoughts Before Sleep

Emotions Before Sleep

Dream

Interpretation

Feeling Upon Awakening

Comments

Deam Journal

Date:__________ Time:__________

Thoughts Before Sleep

Emotions Before Sleep

Dream

Interpretation

Feeling Upon Awakening

Comments

Deam Journal

Date:____________ Time:____________

Thoughts Before Sleep

Emotions Before Sleep

Dream

Interpretation

Feeling Upon Awakening

Comments

Deam Journal

Date:__________ Time:__________

Thoughts Before Sleep

Emotions Before Sleep

Dream

Interpretation

Feeling Upon Awakening

Comments

Deam Journal

Date:____________ Time:____________

Thoughts Before Sleep

Emotions Before Sleep

Dream

Interpretation

Feeling Upon Awakening

Comments

Deam Journal

Date:____________ Time:____________

Thoughts Before Sleep

Emotions Before Sleep

Dream

Interpretation

Feeling Upon Awakening

Comments

Deam Journal

Date:__________ Time:__________

Thoughts Before Sleep

Emotions Before Sleep

Dream

Interpretation

Feeling Upon Awakening

Comments

Deam Journal

Date:____________ Time:____________

Thoughts Before Sleep

Emotions Before Sleep

Dream

Interpretation

Feeling Upon Awakening

Comments

Deam Journal

Date:__________ Time:__________

Thoughts Before Sleep

Emotions Before Sleep

Dream

Interpretation

Feeling Upon Awakening

Comments

Deam Journal

Date:__________ Time:__________

Thoughts Before Sleep

Emotions Before Sleep

Dream

Interpretation

Feeling Upon Awakening

Comments

Deam Journal

Date:____________ Time:____________

Thoughts Before Sleep

Emotions Before Sleep

Dream

Interpretation

Feeling Upon Awakening

Comments

Deam Journal

Date:__________ Time:__________

Thoughts Before Sleep

Emotions Before Sleep

Dream

Interpretation

Feeling Upon Awakening

Comments

Deam Journal

Date:__________ Time:__________

Thoughts Before Sleep

Emotions Before Sleep

Dream

Interpretation

Feeling Upon Awakening

Comments

Deam Journal

Date:____________ Time:____________

Thoughts Before Sleep

Emotions Before Sleep

Dream

Interpretation

Feeling Upon Awakening

Comments

Deam Journal

Date:____________ Time:____________

Thoughts Before Sleep

Emotions Before Sleep

Dream

Interpretation

Feeling Upon Awakening

Comments

Deam Journal

Date:__________ Time:__________

Thoughts Before Sleep

Emotions Before Sleep

Dream

Interpretation

Feeling Upon Awakening

Comments

Deam Journal

Date:____________ Time:____________

Thoughts Before Sleep

Emotions Before Sleep

Dream

Interpretation

Feeling Upon Awakening

Comments

Deam Journal

Date:__________ Time:__________

Thoughts Before Sleep

Emotions Before Sleep

Dream

Interpretation

Feeling Upon Awakening

Comments

Deam Journal

Date:__________ Time:__________

Thoughts Before Sleep

Emotions Before Sleep

Dream

Interpretation

Feeling Upon Awakening

Comments

Deam Journal

Date:____________ Time:____________

Thoughts Before Sleep

Emotions Before Sleep

Dream

Interpretation

Feeling Upon Awakening

Comments

Deam Journal

Date:____________ Time:____________

Thoughts Before Sleep

Emotions Before Sleep

Dream

Interpretation

Feeling Upon Awakening

Comments

Deam Journal

Date:____________ Time:____________

Thoughts Before Sleep

Emotions Before Sleep

Dream

Interpretation

Feeling Upon Awakening

Comments

Deam Journal

Date:__________ Time:__________

Thoughts Before Sleep

Emotions Before Sleep

Dream

Interpretation

Feeling Upon Awakening

Comments

Deam Journal

Date:__________ Time:__________

Thoughts Before Sleep

Emotions Before Sleep

Dream

Interpretation

Feeling Upon Awakening

Comments

Deam Journal

Date:____________ Time:____________

Thoughts Before Sleep

Emotions Before Sleep

Dream

Interpretation

Feeling Upon Awakening

Comments

Deam Journal

Date:____________ Time:____________

Thoughts Before Sleep

Emotions Before Sleep

Dream

Interpretation

Feeling Upon Awakening

Comments

Deam Journal

Date:____________ Time:____________

Thoughts Before Sleep

Emotions Before Sleep

Dream

Interpretation

Feeling Upon Awakening

Comments

Deam Journal

Date:____________ Time:____________

Thoughts Before Sleep

Emotions Before Sleep

Dream

Interpretation

Feeling Upon Awakening

Comments

www.ingramcontent.com/pod-product-compliance
Lightning Source LLC
Chambersburg PA
CBHW072056280526
45788CB00006B/2303
9781086218626